C ple

CW01625417

The Netherlands, Febr. 23th - 2015

Dear Howard!

It really was a great pleasure meeting you in Boquete!

You showed Julia and me the way to start solving Julia's health problems.

Thank you very much for Sonia's book. Very interesting, we both started reading and follow some of her advices.

We wish you all the best, a lot of happiness and health, more than kind & warm regards,

Jos & Julia

Customers are just like regular people

And 99 other eye openers for customer-orientated working

Jos Burgers

ACADEMIC SERVICE

For more information about this edition and other Sdu editions, please contact:
Sdu Customer Service
P.O. Box 20014
2500 EA The Hague
phone: +31 (0) 70 3789880
www.sdu.nl/service

Academic Service is an imprint of Sdu Uitgevers bv

Lay-out: Holland Graphics, Amsterdam
Cover Design: Scherphuis|Snijder BNO
Cover photo: Shutterstock
Print: Drukkerij Wilco, Amersfoort

ISBN: 978 90 5261 6995
NUR: 802/801

Contents

Foreword

It is the job of a newspaper like *Brabants Dagblad* to explain and interpret so that subjects are clear and understandable to everyone. The newspaper should also help the reader gain insight and form an opinion.
When we added a separate section called 'The Entrepreneur', we wanted a columnist to deal with the marketing side who would really suit the role. Without hesitation we turned to Jos Burgers. He has the unique ability to uncover the essence of a subject using everyday, recognizable situations from practice. Always with a message, but always with a smile.

Customers are just like regular people! is a collection of 33 of his stimulating, humorous and very readable columns, which have been published in a variety of media sources, including *Brabants Dagblad.* Through his columns, Jos Burgers holds a mirror up to his readers and encourages critical reflection on everyday practice. He gives advice that people can start using immediately, and concludes each column with three concrete eye openers for customer-orientated working.

If you are like me, after reading this book you will realize that you have much to improve on, but you will also know how you can do this. I am delighted with this collection of columns because it easy to re-read them and let the advice sink in, instead of falling back into old, bad habits. I wish you much customer inspiration!

Henk van der Zee
General Manager Brabants Dagblad

Customers are just like regular people

1

We happened to strike up a conversation at a network get-together. Every inch an entrepreneur, no doubt about it. I asked him what business he was in, and he answered routinely: 'Cold drawn seamless precision steel pipe'. To my somewhat goading question, 'And what makes your customers really happy?' he replied, 'Well, cold drawn seamless precision steel pipe of course!' He could tell I wasn't convinced, so continued: 'Look, you obviously don't know our customers, but it is true that cold drawn seamless precision steel pipe really makes them very happy.'

'Obviously I don't know your customers,' I said, 'but even without knowing them, I can still say that even your customers are just like regular people.' Now it was his turn to look at me in astonishment.
'Well, of course they are just like normal people. But what's your point?'
'All I am saying is that your customers will be extremely happy if they can be sure you will always deliver on time. As agreed.'
'Yes of course, delivery reliability is extremely important. Especially in the case of cold drawn seamless precision steel pipe.'
'And I imagine some customized work when they need it also makes them happy. Knowing that you can deliver something more than the standard cold drawn seamless precision steel pipe if necessary.'
'Definitely, flexibility is also much appreciated.'
'And knowing you will provide a solution in case of an unexpected problem with the cold drawn seamless precision

steel pipe, instead of engaging in pointless talk about how things got into this state.'

He just nodded. 'And you would probably also make your customers very happy by helping them find cheaper and better solutions to their problems. They also like precise and understandable invoices, and are really crazy about quotations they can understand. And they love quick responses to their questions and friendly people on the phone.'

'That all fits exactly,' he said. 'Just like good seamless precision steel pipe ...' There was a brief silence. 'You know my customers better than I thought.'

'There's no mystery there,' I responded, 'Customers are just like regular people.'

'Well ... but what am I supposed to do with my huge stock of cold drawn seamless precision steel pipe?' the entrepreneur asked me in a startled voice.

'You have absolutely nothing to worry about,' I reassured him. 'If you are reliable, friendly, and quick, and are willing to think along with them from time to time, those customers will be happy to take your cold drawn seamless precision steel pipe as well.' 'But what am I supposed to put on the invoice?' he asked.

'Oh, you can pretend you simply delivered a batch of cold drawn seamless precision steel pipe. Customers are used to invoices not mentioning what they have actually bought from you.'

AND WHAT WAS IT FOR AGAIN?
I LIKE TO IMPROVE MY CUSTOMER ORIENTATION. I WANT TO FIND OUT WHAT MY CUSTOMERS *REALLY* WANT
© PAT

Eye-openers:

"Customers love solutions, but prefer not to have a problem."

"The invoice does not usually reflect what you actually deliver."

"Marketing is too important to leave to the marketing department."

Don't mind the mess! 2

'Don't mind the mess,' the manager said as he invited me into his office. The reception desk from where he came to collect me was disorganized, but it was nothing compared to the shambles on his desk and conference table. Not to mention the corners of his office, which were invisible because of the files that were 'temporarily' stored there.
I don't know about you, but when someone asks me not to mind the mess, it tends to draw it to my attention. I see things I probably wouldn't have noticed without the warning. But this was different. Even without the early warning my first impression would have been: 'cluttered, disorganized, and chaotic'. I casually asked him if he had ever thought about a time management course. Yes, he had considered it, but simply didn't have the time. I nodded as if I understood, and was reminded of the lumberjack who is working up a sweat as he tries to fell a giant tree with a blunt axe. When a passer-by asks him if it isn't about time to sharpen the axe, he snaps at him, annoyed, 'Man, I don't have the time! Do you know how many trees I have to cut down today?'

The exterior of your company – your employees, your cars, your products or services – say a lot about its interior. At least, customers have learnt that this is often the case. If you sit down on an airplane seat that has torn upholstery, and you suddenly feel the armrest is more than a little loose, you are likely to glance out of your window. Are the wings attached more solidly? And if you see a research report that contains a lot of spelling mistakes, you will automatically wonder how carefully the study itself was conducted.

One day, I was waiting at some traffic lights in the city of Den Bosch behind a very dirty small van. It isn't unusual to see unwashed cars and buses, but my attention was attracted by the huge letters someone had written on the back of the van with his finger and a great sense of humour: 'I wish my salary would make me this filthy!' I couldn't believe my eyes when I saw that the van belonged to an industrial laundry company. The inescapable conclusion: there was no way that sheets and pillowcases washed by this firm would be clean.

The outside says a lot, if not everything, about the inside. So, when you are looking for new customers, don't forget your office's exterior, your dress, the reception area, the desk, your cars, and your employees. And intervene when necessary, even if it means a discussion will ensue. Visible navel piercings, for example, are absolutely unacceptable, unless you happen to be in the navel piercing business. But even then you should check whether the base is suitable. 'Don't mind the mess' wouldn't work there either.

Eye-openers:

"Employees without a business card are often the most important business card."

"You don't have to be sick to become better."

"You won't get a second chance to make a good first impression."

3 Outsourcing your wife

My wife loves attention, and I am now looking for someone who can take care of that for me. Someone I can trust to do a good job. Of course, the person I will be outsourcing this task to will have to pretend it is coming from me, otherwise it won't work. I wouldn't want to lose her for the world, but all this attention, it just eats up so much time.
Listen, I have already outsourced several things. I have an agreement with the flower shop in town that they will surprise my wife with flowers every fortnight; always on a Friday at five o'clock. Just before the weekend. That is when the attention is most effective. And a friendly direct-marketing agency is going to send her a card in my name every month, saying something like 'I love you', but in slightly different words every time to make it sound genuine. I have also set up some other contracts. The local wine shop will send her a bottle of champagne every year on our wedding anniversary, and Sligro Wholesale will send a Christmas hamper in mid-December.

Now I just need someone to say something spontaneous to her every now and then. So I'm looking for someone who can do that. I don't know if my actions surprise you, but this sort of thing is really very common practice in many companies. In fact, a brochure about 'outsourcing customer care' has just fallen out of a trade journal. In other words, it's about how I can let others take care of my customers. And it's a real yearbook, absolutely full of 'outsourcing parties'. I'm sure you know them. You call your bank, your insurers, or your utility company and you don't actually get them on the phone. No, you are connected to a tape in a national call centre, with a menu containing nothing of any use to you. You wait, patiently or otherwise, for an operator, but once you get through to her, your joy is short-lived. She also proves to be unable to give you the answers you need.

I quote from the brochure in front of me: 'Outsourcing can increase your flexibility, reduce costs, and free up time and attention for the core business of your company.' Let me explain it one more time. There is only one real core business, and that is finding and binding customers to you. The way to do this is by giving them your heartfelt attention. From the board of directors down to the man who drives the van or the receptionist. And when you do that well, you are welcome to deliver your product; energy, telephone units, or a mortgage or two. More and more organizations are discovering this reality, and no longer believe in huge, national call centres and the like. Managers are also judged less and less on results, and more and more on the satisfaction of their customers. If the customers are satisfied, results will follow automatically.

And by the way, my wife wasn't too impressed with the whole outsourcing thing although she did think it was clever. But now she is working on a plan to outsource me entirely. And that, of course, was never my intention.

Eye-openers:

"Providing real attention is not something you can delegate to others."

"The only way to have a friend is to be one."

"If you never lose another customer, your business will increase automatically."

If it wasn't for those customers ...

4

'Hi, how have you been?'
'Fine, you know. Except for work at the store, of course. It is such a shambles there every day.'
'Shambles? Why a shambles? Because of your boss maybe?'
'No, it isn't my boss, although he is impossible too. He refuses to understand how important I am to the store, and that I should be paid a whole lot more. Well, as long as he pretends I earn a lot, I will continue to pretend to work hard. No, the real shambles is created by the customers, of course. They are really hopeless. Take yesterday, for example. There were so many customers we could hardly get any work done. You know, you are stocking up and just when everything is going smoothly, ten to one some customer will come and interrupt you. And ask a stupid question like "Do you also have this jacket in dark brown?" So I tell him, "If they are there I do, but if they are not I don't!"

And do you think they are ever satisfied? Never! Trust me; our customers are such nags they make my mother-in-law look like an amateur. Just the other day, while his wife was trying on something very unbecoming, the husband comes up to me and asks, "Can I smoke in here?" So I say, "You are welcome to smoke here as long as you don't exhale the smoke!"
And last Tuesday. Quarter to six. This lady walks into the store, as cool as you please. Well, she'd better not buy too much, or you won't be able to get her out before closing. I think your office must be a much better place to work.'
'Better? No way. Our office is exactly the same. There I am, working on an internal memo, and what happens? The

phone rings. Guaranteed it is some customer who doesn't even realize he is interrupting your work. No, I sometimes think to myself, if it weren't for the customers you could take the time to give your colleague a decent answer to his question. Or look something up for your boss. Without customers there would be more time for a work conference, or a decent lunch. Without customers you would finally have the time to reply to all your e-mails. Without customers there would also be enough time to file all your stuff properly. And without customers you might get home on time sometimes.

No, as I often say to my colleagues: if it wasn't for the customers, this place would run like clockwork ...'

Eye-openers:

"Artificial customer friendliness is better that real customer unfriendliness."

"Customers pay your salary, for your new car, and your vacation."

"Life is a party, but *you* have to put up the decorations."

5 Reliability

'Sales department, Mary speaking, how can I help you?'
'Hello Mary, Jos Burgers here. I'm calling because I'm looking for a reliable supplier; a company that will simply honour its commitments. Does that sound like your company?'
'Mr. Burgers, I can send you a beautiful brochure. I can assure you that you will rarely have seen such a beautifully finished brochure in your life. The reactions we get to this brochure are great, especially from friends and family. We really went all out for this brochure.'
'That's very kind of you, but all I'm looking for is a supplier I can rely on. Someone who will do what he says. I don't have much use for nice brochures.'
'A supplier you can rely on! You are asking a lot! I'll tell you what, what if I ask one of our sales people to visit you? You'll see that they are all thoroughly trained. And some of them have a great sense of humour. They can drop off the beautiful brochure at the same time.'
'That is very kind of you, but it's not what I am looking for. I just really need a supplier who will deliver on his promises. Who will still take notice of you after you have signed the contract. Who won't be full of excuses about why things didn't work out.'

'Mr. Burgers, we love new customers. That is why we have a welcome gift for every first-time customer. And to encourage customers to come back to us, we also give out bonus points. These points will get you all kinds of stuff that may not be of much use to you, but it is really beautiful.'
'Madam, you can keep your beads and mirrors. The only thing you can do to make me happy is to keep your prom-

ises. That means that we reach an agreement and you just do it. That would be wonderful. Not having to monitor everything the whole time because you do what you promised, as agreed. Is that really so difficult?'
'I don't know if you like good wine, but you are in luck if you do. I can tell you now that all of our customers receive a bottle of wine at the end of the year. And that's not all. Nothing is too much trouble when it comes to keeping our customers happy. We also throw in a calendar every year. Just because we want what's best for our customers.'

'Madam, please be quiet. I will try to explain it to you one more time. I am simply looking for a supplier I can rely on. All I want is some reliability.'
'Reliability, reliability! I'm sure we'd all like that! Most of our customers are satisfied with the discount we give them when there has been a problem. And you know, the best thing of all, we also issue our own newsletter! We do! Every month ... Hello. Hello. Mr. Burgers? Is there a problem with the phone?!'

Eye-openers:

"The best gift you can give to a customer is your undivided attention."

"Reliability is an exceptionally scarce commodity."

"The best way to honour promises is to not promise too much."

Do not deliver what the customer asks for

6

'I was looking for a 40 to 50 horsepower tractor' my neighbor told me. As the seat next to his happened to be empty, I struck up a conversation with my neighbour at his sister's birthday party. His name was Tom. He had been a farmer all of his life in the village of Moergestel, and he was visibly enjoying thinking back to those times. I was immediately fascinated by his great stories, which were full of jokes. I could hardly get two words in, and just as well because as he was telling me, with a beaming smile, about his experiences as a small agrarian entrepreneur, I was reminded of the story about the small Dutch farmer who, for the first time in his life, visits an agricultural fair in the United States. The land where everything (and everyone) is great, or pretends to be. One afternoon, he meets an American colleague who almost immediately starts to brag about the gigantic piece of land he owns. 'I have so much land,' said the U.S. farmer, 'that if I want to drive around it and I leave first thing in the morning, I wouldn't get home before dark.' To which the small Dutch farmer responds: 'Yes, I know what you mean. I used to have a car like that too.'

Tom talked enthusiastically about his forty years in farming. I was reminded of the article I read not long ago about the new phenomenon of the 'care farm', where first drug addicts, but now also managers suffering from burn-out, are very successfully put to work. According to the newspaper story, working on the farm was the ideal way of reviving yourself, thanks to the physical labour and the appreciation you get there. Another great advantage is that you often work with cows and pigs, and they never complain!

Tom probably knew I was in the marketing business, because he was also eager to share his experiences of suppliers with me. 'So, I was looking for this 40 or 50 hp tractor.' I nodded like I had recently purchased my own. 'I always went to the same place. Why go elsewhere if you're satisfied with the service?' I didn't know either. 'So, the salesperson there knows me very well, and after asking me some questions he told me I didn't need a tractor like that. According to him, 35 hp would be more than enough. A heavier tractor would not only cost more than necessary, it could also damage anything behind it.'
'Suppliers back then,' he sighed. 'They didn't deliver what you asked for, but rather what you needed.'

Eye-openers:

"Give a customer what he needs, not what he asks for."

"It is not the customer's job to think up what is not there yet, it is the entrepreneur's."

"Acquiring orders sometimes requires passing up orders."

7 Just normal language

'This is Human Talent Unlimited, good morning.'
'Oh, excuse me; I must have dialled the wrong number. I was looking for a temporary employment agency.'
'Oh, but we are a temping agency, no problem. How can I help you?'
'Well, I'm looking for a competent temp for our reception desk and for things like answering the phone.'
'If you have a moment, I will put you through to the right department. You are now speaking to the Call Centre.'
'Service Support Department, Melissa speaking, what can I do for you?'
'Good morning, I am looking for a temp for our ...'
'Excuse me for interrupting you, but you've been connected to the wrong department. We are the Service Support Department and I presume you want to speak with someone at our Customer Contact Centre?'
'I don't really care, Miss.'

'Good morning, Customer Contact Centre, Bart speaking.'
'Good morning, I'm looking for a temp.'
'Please give me your customer relationship number, so I can look you up in our Customer Relationship Management System.'
'Well, I don't have a number. Is that a problem? I'm not a customer yet, you see.'
'Oh. In that case you shouldn't be talking to us, but to Sales Support. I will put you through.'
'Sales Support, good morning, Leslie speaking.'
'Good morning Madam, I am looking for a competent temp. To man the reception and answer the phone.'
'Well, perhaps you don't know this, but telephone opera-

tors fall under the Human Resources department. But I'm afraid there is no one there at the moment. You see, that particular business unit was seriously downsized recently because our new company policy is to focus more on commercial jobs like Sales Representatives, Sales Managers, and Sales Executives. Operators are no longer our core business. Do you have any special requests regarding the operator?'

'Well, we have many international contacts, so it would be important that he or she speaks some Spanish.'

'Oh, I am afraid that will be very difficult, Sir. We don't have anyone here who speaks Spanish.'

The sudden appearance of the conductor in my train compartment wakes me abruptly, and with a sigh of relief I realize that it was all a dream. Luckily, many organizations and companies still speak normal language; a language that customers can understand.

'Good morning Sir, may I see your travel warrant please.'

'I am sorry, I only have a train ticket. Will that do?'

Eye-openers:

"Talking all the time does not necessarily equal good communication."

"Some people speak from experience; from experience, wise people frequently do not."

"Be sure to let customers do the talking on websites and in brochures."

A dislike of falling down and getting up

8

I have absolutely no problem in working hard. Nevertheless, it feels really good to get away every now and then. Especially if during a short break you can witness the top-notch performances at the Olympic Games in Athens, and I don't mean Heineken's sublime marketing concept, but rather the gold seekers who started the whole thing. Watching them perform I made a remarkable discovery. Top-notch performances nearly always start with falling down and getting up. Or rather, with not wanting to fall or get up. Let me explain.
Take Leontien van Moorsel, the Dutch cycling champion who never falls off her bike. She has always had, and still has, such a dislike of falling that she always wants to be in the lead. The risks are much less there because there is no chance of getting caught up in someone else's pile-up. I'm sure that in the long run this will teach you to ride a bike very fast. And if you do it for long enough, you will automatically become a champion. So, if you thoroughly dislike falling, go and buy yourself a racing bicycle.

Getting up is pretty much the same thing. Dutch athlete Lornah Kiplagat, who is originally from Kenya, represented the Netherlands in the 10 kilometre run. She told *Sportweek* magazine that she had always hated getting up in the morning: 'I was lazy; I always got out of bed very late and consequently had to run to school to get there on time. If I wanted to walk to school, I had to get up so much earlier. I thought: if I run those six kilometres as fast as I can, I can stay in bed that much longer.'
There was only one possible conclusion: the very best way to achieve change, innovation, and improvement, is to

completely abhor something. When I realized one day that I seriously dislike writing long reports, I decided to simply stop writing them. The result? It cost me a job or two, but this loss was offset by the many new customers who were satisfied with one or two pages.
What do you thoroughly dislike? What things are you totally fed up with? These things may turn out to be great motivators for change and innovation. Do you really not like internal claptrap? Simply spend more time on your customers. Dislike winning customers over? Leave it to someone else. Or think up a completely different solution to find new customers. Not every change may work perfectly from the start, but you will see that after a period of falling down and getting up – of trial and error – you will achieve a top-notch performance.

Eye-openers:

"Everyone said it was impossible, until someone came along who didn't know that."

"If you have everything under control, you are not going fast enough."

"Logic will take you from A to B, imagination will get you everywhere."

9 Automated nonsense

Just before the end of the Cold War, Russian President Brezhnev took part in a salute as part of a visit to his American colleague, Ronald Reagan. Tanks, armoured vehicles, mobile rocket installations and armed troops filed past them. Yet, in between all of these army units there suddenly appeared a group of men in business suits and ties, carrying briefcases. The Russian leader asks Reagan: 'What are those guys in the suits doing there?' Reagan's answer: 'Those are all Heads of Automation; you wouldn't believe the damage they can do.'

I don't want to immediately antagonize the entire ICT world; I am not automatically against automating anything, although ICT can take you to the brink of ruin. In 2001, publicly quoted company Hagemeyer N.V. decided to implement a worldwide IT system for its logistical infrastructure. The main effect was customers leaving *en masse* due to the huge delivery problems. The company almost didn't survive.

But there are also many blessings. I would really miss online banking. And ordering books online. It takes me about eight seconds to order my management literature from managementboek.nl, and two days later the books are delivered. What an invention!

I often wonder though whether customers are really interested in solving non-existent or barely detectable problems. Take Miele, for example. The company has reportedly long been working on a washing machine that is connected to the telephone, and will automatically report malfunctions and life span to the service department. Can you imagine: the doorbell rings and there is a mechanic to do the maintenance. 'I'm sorry, but I didn't call you.' 'That's right, Sir, your washing machine did.'

But what really makes me critical is when automation is presented as a Customer Relationship Management (CRM) tool. In my opinion, supporters of CRM are very quick to say that you can use customers' behaviour to sell other products and services, yet this presumes that there is an average customer, who in reality does not exist.
When you buy a book from online bookstore bol.com, for example, more titles are suggested to you under the heading 'People who liked this book also ordered ...' I decided try it out on one of my own books, *Een hogere prijs is pure winst* (A higher price is pure profit). What tips would the computer at bol.com offer the buyers of this marketing text? One of the titles was *Building styles in the Netherlands 1040-1940.* Although the costs of building have undoubtedly risen considerably over the years, this recommendation is pure nonsense as far as I'm concerned. But, fortunately, there was also a second tip. According to the computer, the buyers of *Een hogere prijs is pure winst* also ordered *Alice's Adventures in Wonderland.* And yes, I know that some people feel I'm telling fairy tales, but what is one supposed to do with this recommendation? It's pretty obvious what you get when you automate nonsense. It is most likely to be automated nonsense ...

ISN'T IT A BIT LATE IN THE DAY FOR THE KAMA SUTRA?
IT WAS RECOMMENDED BY BOL.COM WHEN I ORDERED THAT EMBROIDERY BOOK FOR YOU
Kama Sutra
© PAT

Eyeopeners:

"Predicting is difficult, especially the future."

"He who learns from his mistakes will become very successful."

"There is no such thing as the average customer."

10 'I will sell anything except my mother-in-law'

In the distant past, I have tried to explain to groups of high school students how annuities work. No easy task, I can tell you. Not only because I had a bit of a problem with the subject myself, but primarily because they didn't want this kind of information. Those sixteen and seventeen-year old boys and girls had many needs, but an explanation of annuities was definitely not one of them. The reason was simple. Those adolescents simply did not have a problem which could be fixed with annuities. It's not that they didn't have any problems, just none that I had a solution for.
I was actually selling something to someone who did not have a single need for it. I have often thought that this could be the origin of the bad reputation that the 'salesperson' has. Studies into the subject show that few professions score lower than that of salesman. This is probably because of the type who claims he can 'sell anything'. You have seen them, the show-offs who will cheerfully comment at parties: 'I will sell anything except my mother-in-law. Her I'll give away for free.'

Attempts to sell something to someone who does not have or is not experiencing a problem evoke a lot of resistance. That explains the dislike people have of salesmen and women. I recently attended a seminar with management guru, David Maister. He repeatedly said: 'Nobody wants to buy anything, but everybody wants to be helped.' A simple sentence, but profoundly meaningful. Let me repeat it: 'Nobody wants to buy anything, but everybody wants to be helped.' Buying is often synonymous with everything that potential customers dislike: a salesperson who talks a lot and tries to persuade you to buy something he really wants to sell, regardless of whether it will make you, the customer, happy. Or, as Dutch comedian Freek de Jonge remarked so aptly in a show several years ago: a travelling salesman rings a doorbell and says to the housewife who comes to the door: 'Little lady, I have brought you something you have been waiting for for years: nonsense with an extension cord.'

Why don't we start helping the customer? Helping requires putting yourself in the other person's shoes, gathering information about him. You can't help without asking the right questions, the answers to which let you clarify the other person's problem. Only then can possible solutions be formulated. The next time you talk to a customer, start by asking yourself how you can help him. Chances are he will subsequently want to buy all kinds of things from you. Except your mother-in-law, of course!

Eye-openers:

"It is good to be true to yourself, but don't forget to look at things from the other person's perspective."

"Flowers don't grow by pulling on them."

"Profit is like air. Necessary, even essential, but it won't make you happy."

Books nobody reads

11

Many people know me as the man who writes books nobody reads. In my experience, entrepreneurs and managers, apart from a very few exceptions, don't read books. Fortunately for me and many other authors of management books, you do regularly buy them. My request to you, of course, is to please continue buying them in the future. In return, I promise that they will be very thin books, because you dislike thick ones intensely. You never buy those. In the past, I have occasionally tried to please an entrepreneur by giving him one of those thick texts as a present. But even that wasn't easy. He only wanted to accept it after I reassured him that he wasn't obliged to read it.

Entrepreneurs who confide in me that they occasionally read a book are very honest about it. Preferably, it shouldn't be too thick, and should have lots of pictures and even more examples. Oh, and a large font, so it doesn't take too long to read it.
The management bestseller top ten proves it. The prime positions are invariably occupied by books that are OK in terms of content, but are nothing in terms of size. All of you who have read *Who stole my cheese?* will know what I mean.
It must be clear to you by now what I am doing. I'm trying very hard to restrain myself. I know you don't have much time, and you are definitely not waiting for endless stories. What I would really like is to write a 750, or even better a 1000 word story, but I know you won't like that. And so I keep to the 500 words reserved for this column, in the hope that we can make it to the end together. Fortunately, I don't want to force too many messages on you, so let me

begin with the most important one before I've used up my quota. When you communicate with your customers or your target group, make sure you restrain yourself. Limit the amount of text in your brochure, because people won't read it anyway. They might skim through it though, so make sure you put in lots of nice pictures.

And don't overload your website with too much information either. That isn't what people want, and giving out lots of information on it isn't your primary goal. I imagine that you would prefer potential customers to contact you. In that case, it may be wise to hold some details back and pique their interest.
Also, make sure you restrain yourself even more in your sales presentations. This is another instance of less is more. And stop putting so much text in ads and newsletters. Take it from me: it doesn't improve anybody's mood.
So, will you restrain yourself a little from now on? Then I will too, OK? I promise you my next book will be even thinner. And it will have more pictures and a bigger font! Deal!?

Eye-openers:

"Pictures speak louder than words."

"The best way to learn something is to teach it."

"What many people see as good communication is often no more than an attempt to avoid talking at cross-purposes."

12 No options please

I'm pretty hopeless. At least as far as choosing is concerned. I am a Libran, you see, so I don't like to make choices.
'Shall we have a dessert?' 'That's fine!' 'Or maybe we shouldn't?' 'Oh, that's OK too.'
'Do you want to go away for a couple of days?' 'Yes, good idea!' 'Or would you rather stay home this time and relax?' 'Hmm, that also sounds good!'
I sometimes get so tired of being me. And I'm not the only one. Suppliers think I'm a disaster as well, but they have themselves to thank for that. They drive me nuts. I'm connected to the Internet via cable, and was contemplating switching to ADSL. On further investigation, however, I quickly changed my mind. You have to choose between ADSL Lite, ADSL Standard, ADSL Comfort, ADSL Advanced, ADSL Plus, ADSL Special, ADSL Economy, ADSL Smart, and ADSL Family. I can just hear myself on the phone: 'I'll have the regular ADSL, is that an option?' On second thoughts, Internet via cable is not so bad. As a supplier you have to mess up really badly to make your customers leave you.

The only remaining question now is: grey or green power? Additional insurance on top of the basic package or not? Unleaded gasoline in the tank or back to V-power? Fixed price electricity for the next three years or not? Order a regular Coke or a diet-Coke?
The average drugstore carries thirty brands of anti-dandruff shampoo, and you can't even begin to count the variety of the normal ones. So, if you have a dandruff problem you are very lucky.
There used to be three television stations. I talked to someone who had 500 via a satellite dish. When I asked him how

he liked it, he answered that there was often nothing worth watching on TV!

It may seem to be a very customer-orientated thing to offer your clients a great variety to choose from. But it remains to be seen whether this will make your customers happy. It definitely makes them buy less, so research tells us. In his book *The paradox of choice* American psychologist, Barry Schwartz, describes an experiment with jars of jam. Twenty-four different jars were on display in a delicatessen. The next day they put out only six. Of course, the twenty-four jars attracted more attention. Such an assortment! What luxury! But it was difficult to decide which one to buy, and this was reflected in the sales figures. When it came to buying, they sold more jam when only six jars were on show than when the large assortment was displayed.
Perhaps brand loyalty is not so much the result of a strong preference for a specific product with particular properties. If you can blindly reach for the same thing every week you don't have to think or choose. Maybe you aren't in the jam business, and are wondering what this has to do with you. The moral of the story is that customers say they want variety, but they prefer not having to choose. You should, therefore, give your clients the impression that there is lots to choose from, but also make it clear which product you would go for if you were in their shoes. The reality is that the customer prefers not having options.

Eye-openers:

"Offering your customers too many options causes decision stress."

"Brand loyalty often equals not wanting to choose again and again."

"Customers often don't know what they want. Thank heaven."

What is a customer?

13

Unfortunately, I never had the opportunity, but it must have been a wonderful experience to dine there. Restaurant Oud-Holland on Pius Square in the city of Tilburg. To make a reservation you simply dialed 3934.
In front of me is a programme from 1948, which was published on the occasion of the 'Great National Bowling Contest', held between the 2nd and 14th October 1948 in the Wilhelminapark in Tilburg. I happened to get hold of the booklet because my parents used to bowl back then.
I leaf through the advertisements that made its publication possible, and the one for restaurant Oud-Holland immediately catches my eye. Under the heading 'What is a customer?' I read the following story.

"A customer is the most important person in this establishment. In person, via letters or via the telephone. A customer is not dependent on us. We are dependent on him. A customer does not mean an interruption of our work. He is the goal of our work. Serving him is not doing him a favour, he does us a favour by giving us the opportunity to serve him. A customer is not someone we can argue with or match our wit against. No person has ever won a debate with a customer. A customer is a person who comes to us with his wishes. It is our job to fulfil those wishes in a satisfactory manner. For him as well as for us. That is the definition of a customer in our establishment."

Recently, under the auspices of The Customer Care Company, several universities and colleges conducted a survey amongst more than a thousand entrepreneurs. It revealed that one in ten businesses today maintains that it is cus-

tomer-orientated. In other words, 90 per cent still have a long way to go. According to the researchers, the limited progress that has been made in previous decades is partly due to the fact that technological solutions were sought. Since the early 1980s and then later in the 1990s, companies have tried to sort out their internal organization by means of automation systems, under the guise of customer orientation. "It has cost a fortune, but has it actually benefited the customers? Companies do realize how important customer orientation is, but they are choosing the wrong solutions," according to a researcher. "In order to improve results they cut costs and bring in more sales staff. This only affects the front of the organization, and does nothing to change the processes, mentality, and the skills of the staff behind it. This creates the leaky-bucket effect."
Not much has changed in more than fifty years. The phone numbers have got longer, that's all. As have waiting times to be connected. 'All the lines are busy right now'. Who in heaven's name are they talking to, I always wonder. Not to me, because I can't get through.

Eye-openers:

"In principle, discussions with customers are impossible to win."

"The customer is always right. Even when he is wrong."

"If you stop improving, you stop being good."

14 Condoms with two holes

In the past five to ten years, a lot of businesses have had to deal with all kinds of ISO terror. In itself that wasn't too bad. Manuals full of procedures, rules and preconditions were introduced wherever situations were disorganized. Not only did this make the mess look less messy, it also produced less mess. All kinds of built-in safeguards ensured perfect production processes.

The question of whether customers actually wanted the things that were produced in those ISO certified processes was rarely asked. Yet you can deliver the greatest nonsense with an ISO certification, for example, a lifejacket made from reinforced concrete. You do have to do this very carefully, so the manual must clearly state who the next-of-kin can turn to, just in case there is a problem. Even condoms with two small holes ('They are ISO-certified aren't they, darling?') are not a problem. As long as the holes are always in exactly the same spot and are always of the same diameter.
In addition to its many advantages, the ISO-terror also has some downsides. Many of the developed procedures and regulations sometimes make it impossible to really satisfy the customer. And all of those rigidly applied rules do little for their mood.

A while back, I bought a book for a customer who had just become a father to read to his child. Although it would be a while before he could enjoy it, I still thought it was a better idea than pink socks. At the store, I asked the sales-lady to gift-wrap it, and hand me the receipt. She immediately started explaining that the book couldn't be returned.

There had been a mother once who returned one, after having read it, to exchange it for another. Since then, the store had introduced a rule: books cannot be returned. She didn't seem to understand my question about whether accepting misuse by one or two people might be better than punishing every other customer with the implementation of a new rule.

Customers aren't surprised anymore when we manage to deliver a product without problems, or provide a service without a hitch. They want more. Much more. Customised work, a flexible attitude on the part of the supplier, no problems, someone who thinks with them, who anticipates problems, a quick response to a question, or the prompt handling of a complaint.
In other words, customers don't just want us to do things right, they also want us to do the right things. Yet, ever since we've been struck by the ISO terror, many organizations still have so many regulations and procedures that it makes it impossible to 'do the right things'. Perhaps it's high time we slightly de-regulate things again?

Eye-openers:

"He who sows mistrust should not be surprised to reap mistrust."

"It is high time for some organizational 'de-regulation'."

"It makes no sense to continue to do the same things and expect better results."

Tons of fun

15

Yes, every sales manager there agreed with me. Trust, trust, and trust. That was the key to successfully selling your copiers, printers, and fax machines. I asked Frank, one of the participants on the course, whether he trusted his colleagues. 'Absolutely,' he answered without any hesitation. So, I proposed that we first do an exercise outside. I led the way, via a steep flight of stairs, to the conference centre's flat roof. The fourteen men and women standing on the gravel on the third floor looked at me curiously, especially when I pulled out a blindfold and put it on Frank. 'So what are we doing here?' he asked in a semi-relaxed tone of voice. I explained that he would be walking across the flat roof in a minute and that one of his colleagues would probably shout 'stop' when he got near the edge. No problem if you really trust your colleagues, I suggested. Well, Frank turned out not to have that much confidence in them after all. Relieved, he took off the blindfold.

How do you gain the trust of, for example, a potential customer? Many garden variety sales courses say you do this by presenting yourself as strongly as possible. For instance, on the website www.salesonline.nl, under the heading 'sales tips' I read that you should prevent 'hesitation language' and not use words like possibly, perhaps, sometimes, etc.

In fact, the opposite is true. Trust is gained by being honest and authentic, and by occasionally revealing your vulnerable side. I once discussed with a director how we could improve the customer orientation of his organization. After explaining my experience in this area, he asked me if I could do it by using the 'meta-method'. I had no idea what that meant, so I answered, 'That shouldn't be any problem, but you will have to explain to me what this method entails exactly.' He started to laugh and indicated that he didn't really know what the 'meta-method' was either; he had vaguely heard something about it once. I could sense that from that moment on, his trust in me had increased considerably. Now he knew that everything I had told him before could actually be true.

Showing your vulnerability is much more effective than loudly beating your chest. The successful Rabobank commercials, in which Jochem de Bruijn self-mockingly explains 'the Rabobank is a cooperative bank, founded by farmers', rapidly gained the approval of viewers, and the bank received a stream of congratulatory e-mails. You are likely to be taken more seriously, more quickly, when you take yourself a little less seriously every now and then. Not taking yourself too seriously and a little self-mockery are important in gaining trust. And there is one more advantage: if you can laugh at yourself, you will always have fun. I wish you lots of fun today.

Eye-openers:

"If you are always honest to your customers, you will have less to remember."

"Nothing is stronger than the courage to show your weakness."

"The best thing you can become is yourself."

16 In our business

It must have been close to eleven o'clock at night when I got into my car. The hour it took me to drive home gave me the opportunity to reflect on the presentation I had given that evening, and the subsequent discussion that ensued with the assembled entrepreneurs of the city of Haarlem. One sentence in particular stuck in my mind. In the conversations during the drinks afterwards, I received many compliments on my lecture, but almost every time these were immediately followed by the devastating sentence '... but things are very different in my business!'
The man I was having a beer with told me he was in the second-hand car market. He had taken over the business from his father. He had learnt a lot from this evening, he said, 'but in my business it doesn't work like that.'

When the second-hand car market picked up, his business increased; when it fell off he had a problem. No, he obviously did not supply the entire market. And yes, if he were to increase his market share his turnover would also increase considerably. Even in a non-growth market, yes that was right.
I decided to rise to the challenge once again, and asked him how he was different from his competitors. 'We are just very decent car folk,' he said with conviction. I was slightly taken aback and decided to wait before asking how he portrayed that. 'Do you know there is a fantastic market for decent car people?' I asked him. 'Half the country is waiting for decent car dealers.' He steered clear of things like fiddling with the mileage and the like.
I couldn't hold back any longer, and asked him how people could tell that he was so reliable and trustworthy. Well,

first of all he gave a three month warranty. And yes, so did his less reliable competitors. And that was true of pretty much everything he did. 'Yes,' he sighed, 'it is not easy to stand out in our business. I can see what you are saying in other industries, but in our business it doesn't work like that.'

I asked him what would make his customers really happy, but he said that was a difficult question. 'What if,' I told him 'a customer buys a car from you but a month later he really regrets it. For example, there is something wrong with it that you are happy to fix, but he has lost trust in the car. Or, it just did not live up to the customer's expectations. Would you be willing – after deducting the cost of the miles he has driven – to give him his money back?'
'That wouldn't make me very happy,' he responded with incomprehension. 'No, of course not,' I said, 'I understand you would prefer a dissatisfied customer to continue to drive one of your cars. But can you see how it would reflect huge confidence in your own product? Customers love security. You wouldn't have to do much advertising in and around Haarlem. Your customers will do it for you. Things that make customers really happy, like flexibility, reliability, customised work and solving complaints quickly are not related to the business you are in.' I could see his mind working.

Eye-openers:

"The things that make customers happy are pretty much the same across all businesses."

"You don't have competitors, you choose them."

"If you want to be everything to everyone, you will end up being nothing to nobody."

There is no such thing as the average customer

17

Many years ago, author Maarten 't Hart was a guest on a television chat show. He had been invited on to shed some light on his latest book of essays titled *De vrouw bestaat niet* (Woman does not exist). All of feminist Holland came down on him like a ton of bricks. Who did he think he was! As is quite common in the case of heated reactions, these were also rash and ill-considered; 't Hart simply wanted to express his adoration of women by explaining that every woman is unique. There are no 'standard women'; every woman is different. The title of his book should, therefore, be primarily understood as being 'there is no such thing as *the* typical woman'. He was certainly eager to clarify that there is no such thing as 'the average woman'.

Now I know men who have very different thoughts on the matter. According to them, the average woman likes to go shopping and talk for hours on the telephone. And she isn't as adept as he is at programming the VCR and parking the car, but let's not go into that here.
Thinking in averages is dangerous, and can have very unpleasant consequences. For example, tradition has it that during World War II a German general and all his men drowned because he was stupid enough to call in the help of a mathematician and statistician. Because his men couldn't swim, he asked the Dutch teacher who lived in a village on the river how deep the water was there. 'Oh, on average *ein meter tief*,' the good man answered in his best German.

There are also very few average Dutch people. What do they look like? Well, the average Dutch person is about one metre and ten centimetres tall. Men, women, children and babies are, of course, included. As half of our population consists of women, and the other half men, the average Dutch person also has one breast and one testicle. Obviously, you understand that there are very few Dutch people, who are a little over one metre tall and walking around with one breast and one testicle. And if you are ladies underwear company, Hunkemöller, and you were to design a new lingerie line for this average Dutch person, it probably wouldn't be very successful.

Just as there are no average women or Dutch people, there are no average customers. When making every day or strategic decisions it is extremely dangerous to keep your average customer in mind. You don't have one. You do have important and less important clients though. There are those who are very demanding and those who demand far too much. There are extremely valuable customers and good-riddance customers, as well as the positive or critical, and those who always find something to complain about.
The worst thing you can do is treat them all as if they were your average client. For now you know: there is no such thing. Different customers must be treated differently.

Eye-openers:

"You should not begrudge your competition some customers."

"It is not about getting as many customers as possible, but getting as many of the most interesting ones as possible."

"The key to success is to first of all not to try to please everyone."

Speech is only silver

18

How much faith do you have in your doctor? A lot, I presume. If you didn't, you would have long since traded him or her in for a colleague you had more faith in.
But what exactly is the basis for this trust? Not his or her diplomas, I suppose? It may be customary among hairdressers or garage owners, but I have never seen a diploma in a doctor's consultation room. But let's not be difficult and simply assume that your doctor has all the necessary papers, including his 'certificates of cutting proficiency'. Although a few Dutch state secretaries, in contrast to what their resumes said, have been known to have little more than a driver's lcense and a swimming certificate. But let's not get into that here.
In all likelihood, your faith in your doctor is not based on his medical knowledge. I don't know if you can judge whether his diagnoses are correct, but I find that very difficult. And frankly, I feel reassured when my doctor is honest enough to say he isn't sure about something either. That to me is much better than when the doctor gives me the impression he is just guessing.
You probably also don't know how good or bad a student your doctor was. Perhaps it took him many attempts before he finally received his much-desired diploma. I'm sure there are qualified doctors about whom fellow-students said at the time, 'He is never going to make it!' Well he did! And he may be your doctor now.
But for the sake of convenience and your peace of mind, assume that you are lucky and your doctor was a typical medical student at the time. Your trust is then probably based on things like him being a good listener and show-

ing understanding, because research shows that being able to listen inspires trust.

The term 'consultation room' is actually ill-chosen. 'Listening room' is much better. Also, keeping or not keeping promises plays a role in gaining trust, as does how carefully you do your work. Honesty helps. And the ability to put yourself in your customers' or patients' circumstances doesn't hurt either.

Is it so different with customers in your business? If you are a service provider, your customers are often unable to judge your technical performance. They base their faith more on the way in which you work than on the quality of what you provide, and they are perfectly capable of judging this.

Perhaps it's useful to list these factors and critically examine just how self-evident it is for your customers to give you their trust and continue to have faith in your organization.

In any case, there is no harm in transforming your store, showroom, consultation room or other place where you talk to your customers into your 'listening room' as soon as possible. For speech is only silver ...

Eye-openers:

"The best way to convince others is with your ears: by listening."

"You will make more friends by showing an interest in others than by trying to get others interested in you."

"What others entrust us with says more about them than about us."

19 Choose to be chosen

When I say 'HEMA', the chances are that all Dutch readers will immediately think of this department store's signature product and say 'smoked sausage'. Do you have any idea how many of these sausages are sold every year? Half a million? One million? No, many, many more. The answer is ten million a year, i.e. one every second that the stores are open.

On its website www.hema.nl, the organization is invariably referred to as 'HEMA', although as a consumer I only know it as 'the HEMA'.

This HEMA is not only famous for its smoked sausages. Their napoleons ('tompoezen') also sell like hotcakes (an impressive 11 million each year). As do the bras, school supplies, socks, slippers, and thousands of other excellent items. The department store apparently considers it to be its mission to sell quality products at competitive prices. What's more, for many years the slogan: 'The secret of success is doing the regular everyday things unusually well' has hung in the elevator at their headquarters

This approach has brought the HEMA many things. As well as happy customers and excellent results, it was voted best department store in 2003. In the *Elsevier Retail* survey, consumers awarded it a final score of 7.1, which also says a lot about how they value the average retailer.

Not only is there a reason to go the HEMA (smoked sausage or napoleons), there is also a good reason to buy (more) when you are there. Now, its low-energy light bulbs have been named as the best by the *Consumers' magazine*, and before that its hand mixers, battery chargers, electric kettles, and cream cakes all turned out to be winners. A customer needs a reason to visit you, as well as a good reason to buy from you.

Department store Vroom & Dreesman has a problem in that respect. It's always busy, so there is obviously a reason to go there. I suspect it must be the permanently, very clean restrooms. If they ever give out an award for the nicest and most hygienic public restrooms in the Netherlands, then V&D is a key contender as far as I'm concerned. These restrooms are usually located on the top floor, forcing you to go through the entire store to get to them. You and everyone else. Yet, people just don't buy much when they are there. Apparently, there is no good reason to spend more than the 20 cents for the restroom attendant. The products are not very special or particularly cheap, so why should I buy anything?

Think about your own company now. What's the reason for potential customers to contact *you*, and why should they do business with you? I hope you can tell me in about ten words. How do you want to be known and what are you doing to make that happen? If you don't choose who you want to be, you will not be chosen. And if you don't choose, you run the risk of ending up like the Vroom & Dreesman of your field.

Eye-openers:

"The secret of success is doing ordinary things unusually well."

"Choosing is often painful."

"Success is not a coincidence; it is the result of decisions."

Don't listen to customers 20

I used to love it as a child. Going to the V&D department store with my mother and using the escalator there. Against the flow of course. Or rather, against the direction that everyone else was taking. I was always a bit contrary, even as a child. Go up the descending escalator as fast as you can, or run down the one that was going up. Frankly, that still sounds like fun to me, but I suspect I would attract rather more attention than I would care to receive.
The senior executive of the large, listed company Asea Brown Boveri, or ABB, used this metaphor to explain the importance of constantly increasing your competitive advantage. He said that the world around you is in a state of constant change because your competitors aren't sitting still. He compared the situation to walking up a descending escalator. If you stand still you move backwards. If, on average, you walk as fast as your competition, you are standing still. To move forward you must be faster than the escalator going down, be faster than the competition.

As a businessman, there is no getting away from the need to continuously improve. You don't have to be sick to get better. But where and how should you begin? It might seem wise to learn from your customers, but that won't help you much. Do not listen exclusively to your customers; they don't always have the answers. Customers have never asked for anything new, and they can't because they aren't aware of all of the possibilities. Professor Jaap de Smet of the Erasmus University in Rotterdam once had this to say about it: "A customer can't think up what is not there yet, that is the entrepreneur's job." It's not that customers aren't smart enough, it just isn't their business. This

has been shown time and time again. KPN director Michiel Buitelaar, for example, recently said this in an interview in a marketing magazine (*Tijdschrift voor Marketing*): “In 1994, I drew up my first business plan for GSM. Research showed that 98% of the population indicated having no use for mobile telephones. Why use a telephone at the grocer’s? They would phone from home. Mobile phones were only suitable for prostitutes and criminals.”
The ATM is another thing that wouldn’t exist today if it had been up to the customers. Every study revealed that they saw absolutely nothing of appeal in the idea of ‘getting money out of the hole in the wall’.
As early as the start of the twentieth century, Henry Ford said “If I had asked consumers what they wanted, they would have said a faster horse.”

Where do we begin then? The best method is probably to use your CS in a FOTS, i.e. use your common sense in a feet on the table session. You simply ask yourself: ‘What would our customers be totally crazy about?’ One Dutch restaurant came up with the following answer: ‘From now on we will pick up our guests and take them home again free of charge.’ The taxi driver is probably a student working his way through college, who supplements his minimum wage with tips. In any case, business has increased dramatically, and so has the consumption of alcohol. And who knows, perhaps one of these days prices will follow suit.

Eye-openers:

"Winning outside means starting inside."

"Be sure to enjoy the climb, your stay at the top will be brief."

"A pessimist sees a problem in every opportunity. An optimist sees an opportunity in every problem."

21 Weekend in paradise

"A Hugo Boss suit for a cheap department store price. And preferably with pampering and first class service." That describes today's demanding customer to a T, according to a product manager at clothes store HIJ. The customer wants more and more, but for less money.
Grocery chain, De Gruyter, became famous for this a long time ago: 'Better products. *And* a ten per cent [discount]. Only De Gruyter.' There is just one small problem though: De Gruyter went out of business a long time ago. So, the strategy of offering more for less money to attract customers is apparently a disastrous one. It does little for your returns if you keep delivering more and asking less money for it.
Fortunately, there is also a completely different way of exceeding your customers' expectations. How? Simply by not doing more and instead promising less.
Let me give you an example that will also benefit you at home. Your partner (it makes no difference whether male or female), asks you when you are finally going to do that one job. You know, the one you've been putting off forever.

Some shelves need to be put up in the shed you did up last year. All the buckets and other stuff have been in the way for months.
As a promise doesn't seem to cost anything at first sight, you say, 'I'll see if I can do it next weekend.' All you actually promise your partner is that you 'will see', but that is definitely not what was heard. You can guess what happens next.
Do you know what works much better? The next time you say 'Darling,' (it's important to disguise messages like this

one carefully), 'let me be honest with you. As you know I'm so incredibly busy right now that I'm afraid it could be months before I get around to it.'

That may get you ten unhappy minutes, but it's the best investment you've made in years. The following weekend you simply put up the shelves, and I guarantee you will have a weekend in paradise.
Remember that the next time you make a promise. A promise to return a call, to deliver quickly, a promise to prepare a proposal soon, promises to handle a complaint without delay, a promise to ... well, anything you can think of.
At first sight, promises cost nothing, and maybe that is why we make them so generously. But if you aren't careful, they will end up costing you a lot of goodwill and, eventually, customers. Then, of course, there is your relationship at home; when there is such a great option available you can make every weekend a weekend in paradise.

OK, I'LL TRY, BUT I'M NOT MAKING ANY PROMISES!
THEN IT CAN'T BE ALL BAD!
© PAT

Eye Openers:

"Promising less is easier than doing more."

"If you do everything a customer wants, you probably won't last until the end of the year."

"Everything you promise, you are sure to lose."

22 Am I that pale?

Has it ever happened to you? Supposedly independently of each other, your friends pull a prank by kidding you into thinking something. It can go like this: you're at a party, and around nine o'clock number one starts: 'Tell me, have you had a busy week or something?' 'Me? A busy week? No, not really. Why?' 'Oh, you look a little pale, but maybe I'm just imagining it.'

Half an hour later friend number two starts: 'You haven't been ill this week by any chance, have you?' 'No, I've been working and I feel fine. Why do you ask?' 'I thought you looked a little pale, but I must be mistaken.'

About an hour later number three checks in: 'Hey, how are you. Is everything OK? It looks to me like you didn't sleep very well last night!' 'I didn't sleep well? What are you talking about?' 'Well, you don't look very healthy.'

And an hour later: 'You didn't eat something that doesn't agree with you, I hope? 'Not at all, why?' 'You look a little grey to me.'

One more conversation like that and you will be heading for the bathroom to check your colour in the mirror. And yes, now you also have the feeling that you don't look very good. After carrying on for a little longer, you feel increasingly unwell, and go home feeling really ill.

Something similar is going on with customers who want a discount. If you are told repeatedly that you are (too) expensive, you run the risk of starting to think that maybe you are. As a result, you'll find the idea of giving a discount increasingly reasonable and normal, even when there really is no reason to. Customers don't want a discount at all. They just don't want to pay too much unnecessarily, and to make sure they don't, they ask for the discount. Giving it to them confirms that they would have paid too much. Telling them it is impossible reassures them that they are not. The best thing to do is to bear in mind that it is really all a big game. Once, a potential customer asked me to submit a quotation following a productive meeting. Because the atmosphere was right, I asked him if he would be asking for a discount after receiving my quotation, and if so, how much. First, he looked surprised and then started to smile. 'Look,' I explained, 'at this point I can factor in giving you a discount. If I don't, then maybe it won't be possible later on.' We resumed our discussion about rates and reached an agreement on the spot.

Of course, it is difficult when customers tell you that you're expensive. But the real danger is that you will start believing it yourself. So, the next time a customer asks you for a discount just ask yourself: 'Am I that pale?' You now know the answer.

Eye Openers:

"If you are never too expensive, you are probably too cheap."

"Never give a discount without asking for something in return."

"If you are very cheap, you have a lot of explaining to do."

Disappointing your customers 23

The year is 1960. Brothers Ab and Gerrit Heijn (sons of Albert) initiate so-called 'thinking meetings' at the hotel Duin & Kruidberg in the village of Santpoort. Today we would say that they had decided to go on a retreat for a few days for a strategy meeting. They wanted to take the time to talk to each other about the future. Their uncle Gerrit, who thinks it is all a waste of time, is not present at these sessions.

One important subject is the question of how to beat the competition. The market leader is the grocery chain De Gruyter from Den Bosch and, to a lesser extent, Albert Heijn's neighbour in Zaandam, Simon de Wit.

Around 1950, both brothers fell in love with the United States' phenomenon of self-service, but Uncle Gerrit doesn't like it. He is focusing more and more on the production side of the company, and wants to retain his independence from the large manufacturers. He feels that the stores should just sell what the factories produce. The customer should not complain.

During one of the thinking meetings, both young board members quickly agree. They make the drastic decision to say goodbye to the small, traditional grocery stores and rapidly replace them with self-service supermarkets. To pay for the construction work, they decide to sell a few factories. They record their ambitions in a ten-year plan. It is the first ever strategic plan for Albert Heijn. The rest is history. De Gruyter is long gone, as is Simon de Wit. Albert Heijn did almost cease to exist, but for an entirely different reason. If you want to read about the whole story, I heartily recommend the fantastic book *Het drama van Ahold*

(The Ahold drama) by Jeroen Smit. It should be mandatory reading for entrepreneurs and managers.

Last week, at the invitation of a bank, I started working with a group of twenty of its customers. These were twenty entrepreneurs who wanted to hold their own strategies up to the light again. The strategic decisions of the brothers Heijn, and the consequences for the chain and its competitors, were a wonderful illustration to get us started. For strategy is rarely about thinking up totally new and creative things. The point is that you dare to choose from the different options you have. Decide between the opportunities that you are, usually, already aware of. You must want to be 'different' from your competitors. Unique.
According to American management guru Michael Porter, companies too often want to be everything to everyone, whereas it is the strategist's job to disappoint some customers. The Heijn brothers decided to ignore the consumers that wanted to be served. According to Porter, strategy means that you choose what you won't do (anymore), and which services you won't supply (anymore). That is why strategy is so hard.
Ask yourself: 'Which customers are we going to disappoint in the coming year?'

Eye-openers:

"Sometimes you must stand still to get ahead."

'Speed is only positive when you are going in the right direction."

"Strategy is not about doing things better, it is about doing things differently."

24 Pub-crawling Salvation Army soldiers

What is a marketing consultant like me doing in a psychiatric hospital? 'Getting treatment,' you might think. The people who have always thought my ideas were absurd will have no doubts. They have always thought: either *he* is crazy, or I am.' Well, that clears it up: he is!

I don't think so. Some of you will be disappointed, but my regular visits to the psychiatric hospital were completely voluntary. They were intended to provide support to it, instead of the other way around.

Support it with what? Marketing? Well, yes. The purpose of my visits was to drive the hospital management crazy enough for them to embrace the use of marketing in their organization.

Why am I telling you this? To illustrate that marketing is an instrument that can be utilized everywhere to help realize objectives. Not merely to make a profit, although I admit that this is, very often, the goal.

But it isn't in the profit sector is it? Just because the hospital's objectives are very different in nature, it doesn't mean that it has less use for marketing.

Marketing can also offer a helping hand with matters such as securing government subsidies, better occupancy rates, shorter admission times or job preservation. How? By first establishing who your target groups are and putting yourself in their position. Let me illustrate, with a simple example, that this way of thinking is as old as Methuselah (who, according to the dictionary, is 960)!

An eighteen-year-old young man is contemplating ways of finding the money for driving lessons. His parents say he will have to pay for them himself.

The son is a gifted tennis player. He did not inherit this talent from his father, and decides to take advantage of that fact. He invites his old man to play doubles with him at the next tennis tournament. Dad rather likes the idea. On the court dad does what he can. They win the tournament. Dad is intoxicated with joy. And with the beers he was offered afterwards in the canteen ...

In the taxi on the way home, the son explains to his father that he wouldn't have needed to leave the car at the tennis club if he had had his driver's licence ... which could take him a long time to get.
I admit that this is an exaggerated example, but it demonstrates the simplicity of the principle, and so it is all the more remarkable that so few organizations utilize it. Some examples:
An organization in the field of household education announced a training course 'efficient housekeeping' for working women. No one showed up. Why? Those women were much too busy.
The Salvation Army demonstrates how it can be done differently. The organization wants to offer support to those who have fallen through the cracks in society. In a number of cases this is manifested in alcohol abuse and lengthy and frequent bar visits. The Salvation Army soldiers therefore go to the bars to seek out their target group.
You won't hear the figurehead of the Salvation Army in Amsterdam, Major Bosschart, say that she is employing marketing techniques. And she doesn't have to. But the Army is the perfect illustration that financial gain need not be your goal for you to profit from marketing techniques.

Eye-openers:

"If you only have a hammer, every problem will look like a nail."

"Customers never ask for anything new, because they have no way of knowing what the possibilities are."

"If you don't know where you are going, you will probably end up somewhere else."

Nagging toothache

25

'I should have done it years ago'. How often do businessmen say that once the die is cast? They have finally moved into the new building, the employee who opposed every innovation is finally let go, room has been made for more personal leisure time, they have said goodbye to that group of customers who cost more than they bring in, part of the product range has been included or excluded, we have said 'no' to a partner, etc.

I want to talk to you about making choices. Why do we always put off making decisions for as long as possible? Why do we postpone them? I'll tell you why: they give you a toothache because choosing is almost always difficult. Choosing normally means that there is no way back. And when you decide to do something, you automatically also decide not to do something else. This is nearly always a painful decision. If you do not decide, you simply keep your options open and avoid the pain.

I know of almost no situation in which not choosing is better than choosing. Of course, sometimes it's better to put the decision off for a while but only if you don't have all the necessary information. If you can't indicate clearly what information you lack, then there is nothing to stop you making the decision. What are you waiting for?

The fear of making the wrong decision stops us from cutting the tie. Yet in many cases, no decision is actually much worse than a bad decision. Last night I held a presentation for the employees of a thriving technical wholesaler. A company which twenty years ago was a hardware store that also sold stoves and toys. You can imagine what would have happened if nobody there had ever made a clear decision.

Making the decision often brings great relief. That is because you are permanently rid of your toothache. And as a rule, your employees will be very grateful. Clarity at last. And your partner also won't know what is happening to him/her. You are sleeping as well as you used to and, therefore, so are they.
Of course it's easy for me to say this. As a consultant I don't have to make the decisions. I tell my customers what strategic options they have, what the consequences are, and which decision is, therefore, the obvious one to make.
It doesn't really matter too much which decision is ultimately made, as long as one is. My practice has taught me that an informed decision, based on information, facts and common sense, quickly makes the toothache go away. Only then will there be enough room in your mind to see new and interesting choices.

Eye-openers:

"A bad decision is better than no decision. You can learn from your mistakes."

"Regret is usually about things you didn't do."

"If it is free, it's a suggestion.
If it costs money, it's advice.
If it works, it's a miracle."

26 Having no idea

Ignorance can be such a wonderful advantage. Not knowing anything about a particular subject. Not being hindered in any way by the slightest amount of knowledge. In that situation anything is possible! That's the beauty of it. Let me explain. Late in December, I received a holiday card with the maxim 'Everyone said it was impossible, until someone came along who didn't know that.' Now I have no intention of playing the philosopher here, but if you read that top-class phrase again you will discover that, apparently, it can be a huge advantage not to know something. For then there are no limits. Good news, right?

'Everyone said it was impossible, until someone came along who didn't know that!'

So everything is possible! The major limitation on our creativity is our own limited thinking.

When I'm with customers, I often discover that they no longer see their own potential and market opportunities. They don't see the problems heading their way, nor the wonderful opportunities, let alone the very ingenious solutions.

An example. Take your newspaper, the daily you see every day. Question: are you happy with it? If not, what exactly are you unhappy about? Think about it for a minute.

Now, I want to ask you to give an honest answer to the question of whether you are enthusiastic about the format of your paper. Have you ever tried to read it on a train or an airplane? Excuse me? Not very handy? And yet that thought probably didn't enter your head when I put my first question to you.

Any random European from a country that does not have our unwieldy newspaper format immediately exclaims upon seeing our mega-sized papers, 'What is this abnormally large and unmanageable thing? Why would you Dutch people want that?' And so I explain that we aren't too happy about it either, but we just don't see it anymore. What are you supposed to do with this example? Well, what I want to demonstrate is that it is sometimes worthwhile switching off your knowledge when you look at your business. I know, it's not easy, but if you want to develop a helicopter view it's very useful to not see too many limitations. Just have the courage to dream; to let go of reality.
If this is difficult for you, let others do it, and not necessarily a consultant. Ask your acquaintances about your business. They are unbiased and open-minded about your market, your strategy and your organization. Or really listen to a new employee before he is also no longer surprised by everything he sees. For that happens very quickly. Try not to explain immediately why something is like this or like that, but ask yourself whether everything you do really makes all that much sense.
Knowledge is power, but not having too much knowledge is also really great.

Eye-openers:

"An idea that is not absurd initially has little chance of being successful."

"High budgets kill creativity."

"If you want to be creative, it helps to have a problem."

Get yourself some chickens 27

I often feel a bit sorry for entrepreneurs. Another successful fiscal year has passed, but the average businessman has trouble enjoying it. Indeed, his focus is already on the new year. 'Starting from zero again' is the slightly concerned comment.
What is true of investing, apparently, also applies to entrepreneurship: 'Past results do not offer any guarantees for the future.'

The question, however, is whether this is actually true. In other words, if this is the case aren't we doing something very wrong? Compare the turnover, or orders or assignments you want to acquire to eggs. You then have two options. You can go out and look for eggs every day, but there is a more efficient way. You can also get yourself some chickens: strong, lasting and loyal relationships.
Yet, this will only work if you exceed their expectations on a regular basis. Real chickens are more than happy with you. They recommend you to others, they sing your praises! But then, that is the type of chicken that is of some use to you. Price barely influences real chickens; they buy more and more as well as more often from you, they provide free advertising for you and they are loyal to boot. And perhaps your relationship is so strong that they tell you for free how you can improve your business even more.

How many of these chickens do you have? How does it show? Would you like to have more of them? If so, how and where to begin? Maybe you are already too busy right now to satisfy all of your customers, let alone exceed their

expectations. You simply lack the time, money, and manpower to give them a little extra.
The solution is amazingly simple. Make a clear decision and determine which customers do and which customers don't have to become strong business relationships. Who do you want to have and hold as a chicken? Who can you miss out? Not every potential relationship is equally interesting. And I assume you prefer fertile chickens, don't you? Not those mid-life chickens that may decide to lay an egg at some, undetermined, point.

This means that your entire organization will have to be geared towards pleasing and pampering your significant relationships, i.e. your chickens. Everybody needs to know who they are and what special treatment they deserve.
Make sure to ask yourself who really deserves this special treatment. Only invest in real chickens, and the eggs will come automatically. Wouldn't it be great if you could say from now on: 'Past results guarantee a very bright future for me'?

WE'VE GOT THE CHICKENS, BUT STILL NO TURNOVER. MAYBE WE NEED TO ADD A ROOSTER...
OR MAYBE YOU JUST NEED TO READ THIS BOOK MORE CLOSELY
© PAT

Eye-openers:

"Some customers are simply more right than others."

"All customers are important, but some are more important than others."

"Why treat different customers the same?"

The end of the Stone Age 28

Two questions. When did the Stone Age end? And why? No, this isn't another science quiz. I would like to ask you to put your feet up on your desk and contemplate your distant future for a moment. Your distant business future, that is.
Let's go back to the Stone Age. Why did it end at some point? According to the history books, it didn't end because the stones ran out. The real reason is that some prehistoric Gyro Gearloose discovered that it was much easier to make tools and weapons from bronze. After he first discovered bronze, of course, which was quite a feat in itself. Once the first Neanderthals quickly realized that bronze has many advantages over stone, the rest of the market followed bit by bit. And in time, any caveman worth his salt no longer wanted to be caught dead with weapons and tools made from stone.

That also answers the question of when exactly the Stone Age ended. It is as good as impossible to say. Not because there are no witnesses left, but because it is simply not possible to pinpoint an actual moment. Not even a year. Not even a particular century. For a change in demand takes place agonizingly slowly and quietly, but very surely, nevertheless. The same happened with the demand for carbon paper, tape recorders, coffee grinders, tea-cozies, coal, Solex mopeds, television antennas, ink bottles, typewriter ribbons, hand drills, etc.
So, what am I supposed to do with this information, you no doubt wonder. Well, it's important that you build up a position in bronze before the demand for stone stops altogether. It is of the utmost importance that you gain experience with bronze, hold on to customers and secure a

position in the market, just in case you can't make a living selling stone anymore.

What do you need to do? Start by determining what is bronze and what is stone in your field. Then analyze the past year. How much business did you do in the one, how much in the other? Then set yourself a clear target. What percentage of your business do you want to do in bronze in the coming year? And then the toughest question. What are you going to do to realize this? Write half a page. Who is going to do it? How are you going to encourage them to do it? What is your core strategy? What means and resources are you going to use? And which cavemen are you going to start with? Who is already starting to get a kick out of bronze?

Know that it is best to change before you really have to. When you really have to it may be too late. And you may think you have some very loyal cavemen right now, but as soon as your competitors start waving the bronze around, the temptation may prove to be too much.

Eye-openers:

"When it is necessary to change, it is often too late."

"Every market will automatically lose its appeal. Slowly, but very surely."

"The only thing that does not change through the years is the need to change."

29 Did you lock your back door?

It was unfair. Simply not right. And it made me so angry. My parents used to be members of the KRO broadcasting network, and so they also had a subscription to the KRO programme guide. As a young boy, every time I leafed through this guide I would run into the same advertisement I took such exception to: if you signed up, you would receive a welcome gift. And not just any gift! No, a pretty set of shiny spoons. Eleven in total. And each spoon had a different provincial coat of arms on it.

It was our bad luck that we already had a membership. In my young boy's mind we had had it forever, and so we were not getting anything. I was jealous of all of those families who were not KRO members because that meant you would be pampered.

I briefly nursed the naughty plan of cancelling our subscription and then reapplying that same week. The guide would be delivered as usual and my parents wouldn't notice.

I didn't do that because I sensed it would be cheating. The KRO did not have those spoons made for us loyal members, but rather for new members.

Today, many businesses do things in pretty much the same way as the KRO did back then. Loyal customers rarely see or hear anything besides regular deliveries and invoices. It's as if being and remaining a customer is totally routine.

Well, it isn't for the customer. Not by a long shot. Research has shown that many customers leave their supplier because they feel ignored. They are rarely, if ever, given any extra attention, and they don't hear much from the company.

More and more organizations have come to realize this, and have decided to start pampering their loyal customers.

Every self-respecting airline company, for example, has its own frequent-flyer program these days: loyal customers are rewarded with presents and free tickets.
Hotel chains have also discovered this particular instrument. They have the so-called frequent-stayer programs to reward and bind their regular customers to them. Through free stays, free use of the fax or telephone, free parking, free morning newspapers and a lot of personal service, they try to cultivate (even more) loyalty in their regular guests.

Aren't those customer relationship management programs expensive? No, they just bring in money. The costs of holding on to a customer are often only a fraction of the costs required to turn a prospect into one. And so it is absolutely worthwhile for entrepreneurs to think about whether it would make more sense to use part of the funds for attracting new customers for holding onto existing ones instead. If you are going to stand at the front door to lure new customers in, it would be nice to know that the back door is locked.
It takes enormous effort (and therefore money) to get any customer you lose to come back.
By the way, I visited my mother this afternoon. She still has the KRO guide. And I wouldn't be surprised if her 40th KRO membership anniversary was coming up very soon. She doesn't know exactly, and neither does the KRO, probably. So I'm very curious to see if she will be getting something on that memorable week. I suspect she will: the guide in the mail.

Eye-openers:

"Acquiring a new customer is many times more expensive than holding on to an existing customer."

"There is not much point in advertising at the front door if the back door is wide open."

"You can shear a sheep many times, but you can only skin it once."

Absolutely PowerPoint-free! 30

I was seated at the front of the hall, waiting for my turn. I was the programme's last speaker, and would have to be patient for another thirty minutes. My presentation was about the issue of what makes customers really happy. It was almost four o'clock in the afternoon by now, and the people at the conference had already had a long day. It had included hundreds of PowerPoint slides. I realized that they were going to be my 'customers' in a little while, and that what would make them really happy right now was a drink.

But they wouldn't be getting one anytime soon. Before me, an engineer from a prominent scientific institute mounted the platform. His talk was about the theoretical life span of sewage pipe. He had twenty-five minutes. And thirty-three slides, as it turned out. By slide number seven the room started to groan, and not with excitement. His main conclusion, that sewage pipe will last longer if you simply leave it in the ground and don't touch it, was crushed between all those slides with their diagrams, calculations and research results. He explained everything extensively. Everything you were already looking at. And also everything you did not see. When his twenty-five minutes were up, he had arrived at slide number nine and the chairman was getting a bit nervous. Another thirty minutes later, having reached slide nineteen, the chairman stood up and pointed at his watch. Three slides later he urged the speaker to speed it up. To the great relief of the room the speaker indicated he would skip a few slides: 'Because they aren't all that important anyway.'

I recently saw the first announcement of an 'absolutely PowerPoint-free' seminar. Apparently the victims are starting to resist. And rightly so. If you want to convey a message you should be aware that you will be more successful if you limit the amount of information. In other words, presentation is selection. Some speakers might as well let their PowerPoint presentation do the work and find a seat at the back of the room.
This art of selection also applies to your sales talks, the presentation of your plans, your brochures, websites, direct mailings, quotations and your letters. In short, it applies to all of your means and methods of communication. It will improve each of them, and make you reach your goal better and quicker.

By the way, this tip can also be used at home. Perhaps you have plans to finally put the holiday photos in an album one of these days. Start by throwing a lot of them away. Do this even if you are a fine photographer, but especially if you are not. The photographs you keep, especially the fairly good ones, will receive a lot of attention and become better for it. Your friends and acquaintances will be very pleasantly surprised.

Eye-openers:

"Presentation is a matter of selection and elimination."

"If you forget to prepare, you must be prepared to be forgotten."

"It takes one hundred muscles to look surly; it takes only twenty to smile."

31 Football without a goal

The more I think about it, the stranger it seems. During a normal football match, the average player is on the ball for a maximum of four minutes. The whole afternoon or evening, that is. The twenty-two players only have ninety minutes to divide amongst themselves. And if you take into account the many time-outs, plus the fact that certain players claim the ball a lot, then no more than two or three minutes of actual playing time is left for some of them. Frankly, there are some players for whom that is more than enough, but let's not get into that here!

Former Dutch national coach, Rinus Michels, made the following well-known statement: 'Football is War'. An American marketing guru became famous with the comment: 'Marketing is War'. If we follow the laws of logic, we may conclude that football is, therefore, marketing.
There is at least one major similarity. In both cases, the objective is to reach the goal. And in football teams as well as in companies everybody contributes a little bit. One major advantage of the sport of football is that you can actually see the goal. The only thing you must remember as a player is in which goal *not* to score.
Even though individual players may not come up to the mark in terms of goal orientation, as a collective they are able to focus so strongly on the goal mainly because they can see it standing right there! This goal has a fixed position and it is hard not to see it. That is to say harder than one of those small checkpoints along the Dutch 'Elfstedentocht' skating marathon. This goal orientation prevents the footballers from simply passing the ball to each other and looking at the stands when they don't have it.

Do your employees have such a clear sight of the goal? Or do they not have any idea where the goal is? Some companies don't want their players to know what the goal is. 'They were hired to play football and if they just shoot at the goal often enough, we will automatically score,' is the reasoning of the management.

In more and more companies, however, people are becoming aware that giving the employees one or more concrete goals is advantageous. Sometimes they go even further and visualize the goal: a glass container in the hallway, put ping pong balls in it and it is immediately clear what the goal is and how far we still have to go.

All day long, your 'players' make small and big decisions, set priorities, pay more or less attention to particular issues, communicate with customers and inform co-workers. In short, there are scoring opportunities throughout the day. But you can only really score if you know where the goal is.

Eye-openers:

"Many people shoot first and then call whatever they hit the goal."

"A dream becomes a goal as soon as you start to take action to realize it."

"Some employees are such soloists; they even prefer to work together on their own."

Success guaranteed? 32

Insurers. Deep in our hearts we entrepreneurs always envy them a little. You set a nice insurance premium, and if it turns out that it is not enough you simply raise it. Of course, there is competition, but we policyholders always tend to feel that they are all the same. And the core business of insurers is absolutely fantastic. Making customers pay for something they do not want at all. The customer isn't chomping at the bit to call his insurer because of a fire, an accident, disability or death.
I'm assuming that you don't sigh to your partner on December 31st: 'Oh darling, the year is up and our house didn't burn down, again; we've paid all of those premiums for nothing, again.'

That is the best thing about insurance. Customers pay for something they don't get. And even better: something they don't want to get. Many entrepreneurs have figured out by now that customers really like security. Guarantees. And that by offering a little security, you can ask more for your product or service. For that reason alone, producers of leading brands can set a price premium.
Entrepreneurs often think that giving guarantees is not for them. But with just a little imagination, anyone can pretend to be an insurer. Transport company Schenker, for example, introduced an 'on-time service'. The principle is simple: late delivery, money back. I know of an ICT company that asks its customers to give them a grade between zero and ten after concluding a project. If that grade is below eight, they will continue to work until the project finally does reach that score, without any additional cost to the customer! Car tyre company Kleber gives a three-

year service warranty on a new tyre. Any car that has tyre trouble in Europe will be helped by Kleber within the hour, free of charge, twenty-four hours a day, seven days a week. A number of driving schools are offering a 'driver's licence guarantee'. I can assure you, you can do more than you might think.

What kind of certainties can you offer your customers? If you do see possibilities, be sure to select something that doesn't cost too much. I once asked the director of a company that produces luxury gift items why he didn't give a one-year guarantee on his products. He answered that there would be little point because not much could go wrong with his products in the first year. I explained to him that that is exactly the essence of a guarantee. If you are afraid that masses of customers will come knocking on your door demanding their money back, you should think twice before giving out guarantees.
Customers are willing to pay for security. And success is therefore guaranteed, although I can't give you any solid guarantees of that!

Eye-openers:

"Nobody wants to buy something, but everyone does want to be helped."

"Many consumers say they never watch commercials, they only buy well-known brands."

"Customers are willing to pay if you are willing to take over their risk."

33 We have been supplying 'SJIT' for years

Maybe you aren't sure whether you want to read this column. It will cost you three minutes of your life and you already have so little time, even before you go to sleep. If you decide to continue, which I obviously hope you will, those three minutes are spent and will not return.
Time is a scarce commodity and scarce commodities are expensive. As the amount of time we have decreases, we are willing to pay more for it.
Some entrepreneurs recognize and eagerly respond to this. Whereas consumers used to have little time to cook a meal every day, it is increasingly common that they even lack the time to get a take-away. The take-out centres of Chinese restaurants (an exaggerated name for three chairs packed together) do less and less business. Pizzerias have decided to no longer wait for the customer to come and pick up something to eat. In many large cities, pizza couriers now take care of the transport; at the expense of road safety by the way, because if a pizza has to stop eight times at a traffic light, it will be cold when it arrives.

In this way, entrepreneurs try to make money by saving you some time. But not all are successful. Many post offices and banks, for example, installed ATMs to help solve the endless waiting inside. The only difference is that now you have to wait in line outside.
Many companies in the business-to-business sector have also discovered time as a 'critical success factor' and as a way to gain a competitive advantage. They focus on fast delivery, but also and especially on delivering at exactly the right moment: just-in-time, or JIT.
An example: say that an assembly department at DAF

Trucks needs 5000 rivets every day. They have an agreement with a supplier to supply the required amount every morning.
The advantages for DAF Trucks are evident. It is no longer necessary to keep rivets in stock, which saves interest, space, and therefore also money. But what about that poor supplier? Don't worry, he also profits from it. Thanks to the long-term contract he has with DAF Trucks, his sales are guaranteed for a significant period of time. In addition, DAF Trucks has reduced the number of rivet suppliers it does business with, so our supplier sells more at better margins. Plus, he can reduce his own stock because he knows the production planning at DAF Trucks. In this way, a much more cost-effective system of doing business has been developed in the entire industry.

It is crucial that deliveries are actually just-in-time. Sooner is too early, and later is too late. Apple, for example, fines its suppliers if they deliver earlier than agreed. And you can imagine what happens when delivery is late! To have their trucks waiting for the delivery of the engines is obviously just as annoying for DAF Trucks as waiting for the screws needed for the engines' suspension. To say nothing of wrongly delivered screws. So, the implementation of JIT delivery has major consequences for the quality you deliver. Faulty products are absolutely unacceptable, return shipments are a disaster and so the demand is: zero defects. Absolutely no mistakes.
In the future, increasingly greater demands will be placed on suppliers. Reliable and just-in-time delivery will be the order of the day more and more often. So there is a lot of work to be done by those companies that are used to delivering SJIT: Sometimes Just In Time!

Eye-openers:

"Kill routine before
it kills you."

"The aftertaste of poor quality lingers much longer than the sweet taste of a low price."

"Quality is hitting the mark every time instead of using shot and hoping a rabbit will come hopping by."

About the author

Jos Burgers RM (1951) studied business economics at the University of Tilburg, specializing in Marketing Management. For a period of ten years, he held sales and marketing positions in a technical wholesale company. After that, he spent more than ten years teaching marketing at Fontys University of Applied Sciences in Eindhoven.

As a marketing consultant and marketing trainer since 1995, he has guided and consulted for companies and institutions of different types and sizes in the areas of strategy, marketing, and customer orientation. In 1999, the Netherlands Institute of Marketing NIMA appointed him Register Marketer (RM).

Jos Burgers is the author of several marketing bestsellers, including *Industriële marketing* (Industrial Marketing; co-author Frans Kense,), *Relatiebeheer als Groeistrategie* (Customer relationship management as a growth strategy), *Een hogere prijs is pure winst* (A higher price is pure profit), *Marketing voor op het nachtkastje* (Marketing for on the nightstand), *Professionals & Customer relationship management*, and *Zeven marketingwetten voor professionals* (Seven marketing laws for professionals; co-author Frank Kwakman).

In addition, he also writes columns for various management journals, and is the author of the marketing columns in the *Brabants Dagblad* newspaper.
Giving over one hundred presentations a year, Jos Burgers is a popular speaker at seminars and conferences.

For more information see www.burgersmarketing.nl.

Acknowledgement

Most of the columns included in this book were published (in Dutch) in magazines and newspapers. The most important are the newspaper *Brabants Dagblad* (section 'The Entrepreneur') and the business magazine *Netwerk Midden-Brabant.*

Several of the columns were partly rewritten and/or updated for this book.

Four of the columns in this volume were also included in the book *Marketing voor op het nachtkastje* (Marketing for on the nightstand).